# Crochet Cat Bed
## Cozy Cat Bed Crochet Patterns

Copyright © 2022

All rights reserved.

**DEDICATION**

The author and publisher have provided this e-book to you for your personal use only. You may not make this e-book publicly available in any way. Copyright infringement is against the law. If you believe the copy of this e-book you are reading infringes on the author's copyright, please notify the publisher at: https://us.macmillan.com/piracy

# Contents

Round Cat Bed made with Jumbo Yarn ............................................. 1

Super Bulky Crocheted Cat Bed ...................................................... 8

Tabby Chic Crochet Cat Bed ........................................................... 17

Super Big Chunky Crochet Yarn Cat Bed ....................................... 24

Crochet Cat Bed for a Comfy Kitty Nap ......................................... 27

Cozy Crochet Cat Bed ...................................................................... 32

Perfect Crocheted Cat Bed .............................................................. 41

Crochet Fluffy Dreams Pet Bed ...................................................... 45

Crochet Cat Cave ............................................................................. 52

# Round Cat Bed made with Jumbo Yarn

MATERIALS:

2 balls Bernat Maker Big in the Amber colorway

US Size N/15 10mm crochet hook (try this one!)

Scissors

Yarn needle

Stitch marker

Heavy books (optional)

ABBREVIATIONS:

Ch = chain

Hdc = half double crochet

Inc = increase (2 hdc in same st)

MR = magic ring

Sc = single crochet

Sl st = slip stitch

Spike = sc in the base of the sc one row below

St(s) = stitch(es)

NOTES:

As you're crocheting the base, your piece may start to cup or curl. If this happens, steam it with an iron or garment steamer and lay a book on top of it to flatten it. Allow to dry, then continue.

When adding your second ball of yarn, drop the current working yarn when you have 4" left, and complete the stitch with the new ball of yarn. This will prevent any obvious knots.

Parts of this pattern are written in crochet shorthand. For example "hdc 2" means to hdc in each of the next two stitches while "hdc 3" means to hdc in each of the next 3 stitches.

## BASE

Round 1: Hdc 8 in MR, pull tail to close ring. Continue working in a spiral. Place stitch marker in the last stitch of the round and move up at the end of each round. (8 hdc)

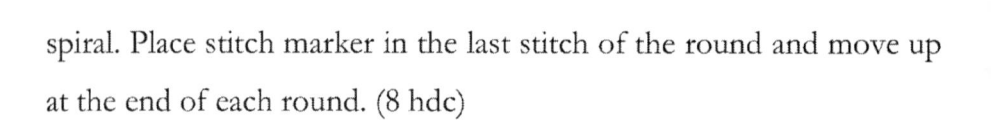

Round 2: Inc in each st around. (16 hdc)

Round 3: (Hdc 1, inc) around. (24 hdc)

Round 4: (Hdc 2, inc) around. (32 hdc)

Round 5: (Inc, Hdc 3) around. (40 hdc)

Round 6: (Hdc 4, inc) around. (48 hdc)

Round 7: (Inc, hdc 5) around. (56 hdc)

Round 8: (Hdc 6, inc) around. (64 hdc)

## SIDES

Round 1: Sc in back loop AND 3rd loop of the next 63 sts. Place 2 sc in the next st. DO NOT JOIN – continue to work in a spiral and move maker as needed. (65 sc)

Round 2: (Spike 1, sc 1) around for 64 sts, spike in last st. (65 sts)

Rounds 3 and 4: Continuing to work in a spiral, sc each spike st and spike each sc.

Round 5: Sl st loosely in each st around. Finish with an invisible join.

## FINISHING

Weave in any remaining ends.

## Super Bulky Crocheted Cat Bed

Supplies:

* Cotton jersey knit fabric, 4 yards white patterned and 2 yards solid red (or your favorite contrasting colors) ** yardage is based on 60" wide fabric

* Scrap piece of yarn, 2-3" long (to use as a stitch marker)

* A small cushion or pillow for the bottom of the cat bed (optional, but it's a nice touch)

# Crochet Cat Bed

Tools:

* Large plastic crochet hook, 15.75mm (US size Q)

* Crochet hook, size K (to help you weave in ends)

* Ruler

* Fabric scissors or rotary cutter and cutting mat

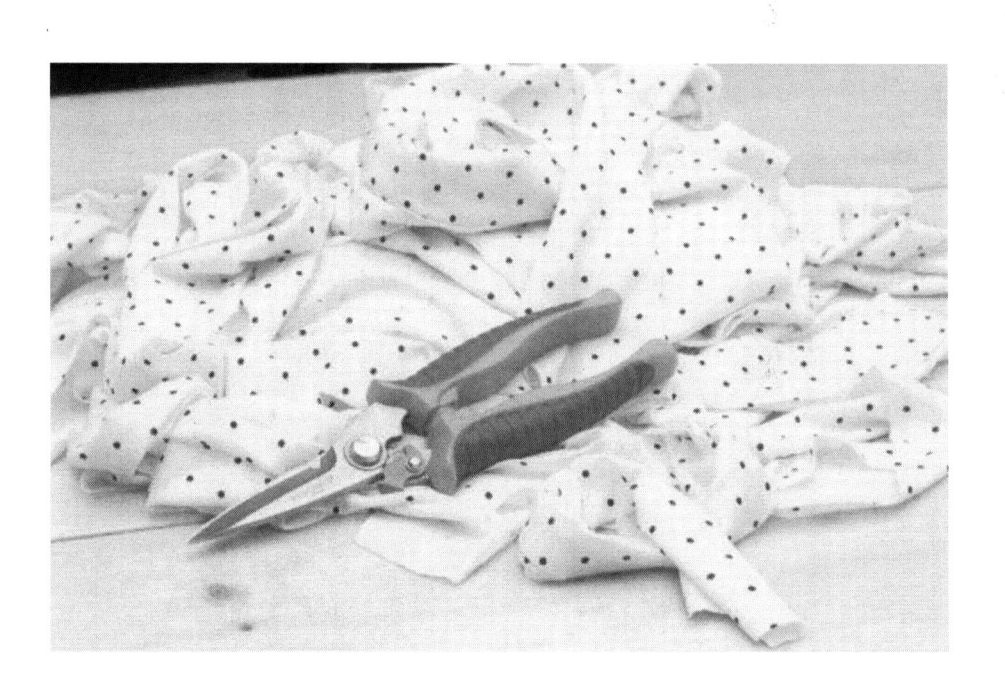

## Step 1

Cut the jersey fabric into long strips that are about 3" wide.

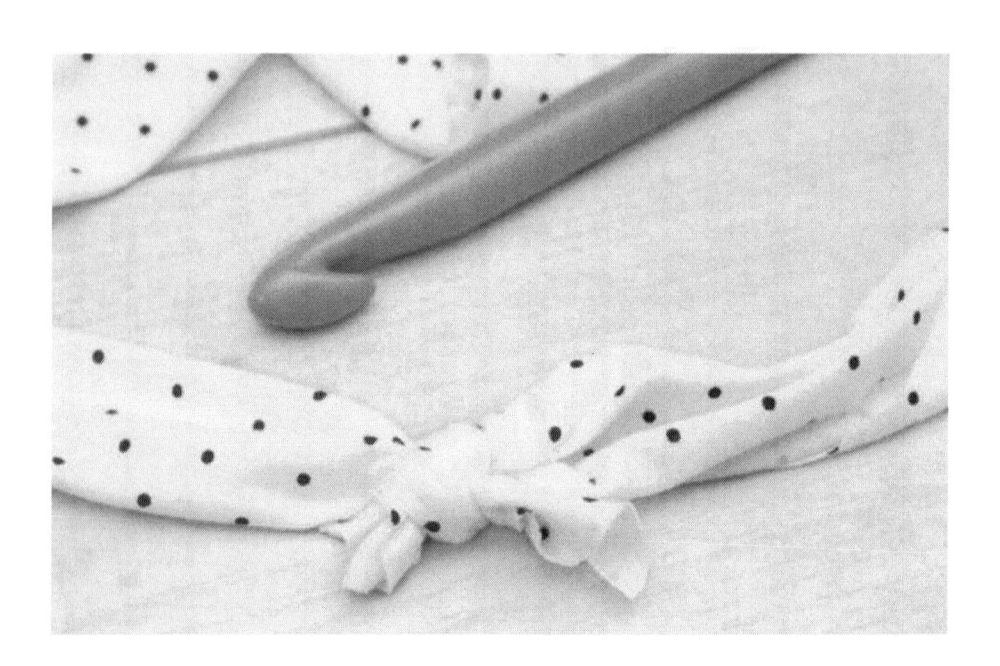

## Step 2

Tie the fabric strips together to make a ball of fabric yarn.

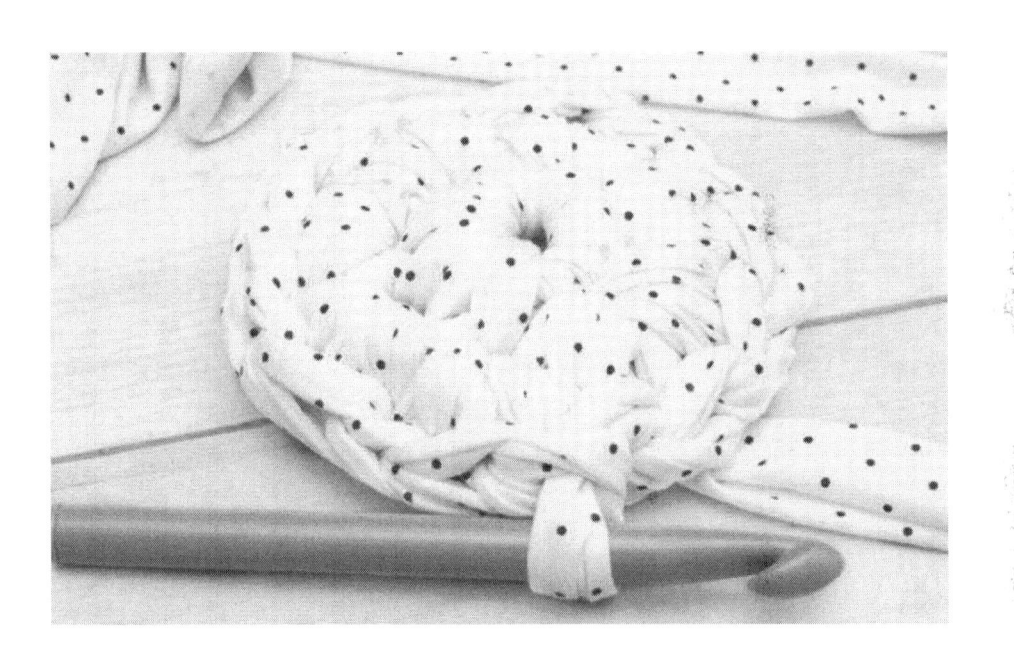

Step 3

Crochet the cat bed using the pattern below.

Tip: Use a scrap piece of yarn as a stitch marker to mark the first stitch in each round.

## Super Bulky Crocheted Cat Bed

Pattern abbreviations:

ch: chain

sc: single crochet

sl: slip stitch

st: stitch

Ch 3 and join with a sl st in first ch.

Round 1: Ch 1, work 8 sc in ring, sl in first sc to join. (8 sts.)

Round 2: Ch 1, work 2 sc in each sc, sl in first sc to join. (16 sts.)

Round 3: Ch 1, *work 2 sc in sc, sc in next sc; repeat from * around, sl in first sc to join. (24 sts.)

Round 4: Ch 1, *work 2 sc in sc, sc in next 2 sc; repeat from * around, sl in first sc to join. (32 sts.)

Round 5: Ch 1, *work 2 sc in sc, sc in next 3 sc; repeat from * around, sl in first sc to join. (40 sts.)

Round 6-11: Ch 1, work 1 sc in each sc, sl in first sc to join. (40 sts.)

Round 12: With contrasting color, Ch 1, work 1 sc in each sc, sl in first sc to join. (40 sts.)

Round 13: Work 1 sl in each sc, sl in first sl to join. Fasten off and weave in ends. (40 sts.)

Step 4

Untie any visible knots in the fabric and weave in the ends using the smaller crochet hook.

Crochet Cat Bed

Step 5

Add a comfy cushion to the bottom of the cat bed and give it to your favorite kitty!

# Tabby Chic Crochet Cat Bed

Level: Easyish

Size: 17" wide x 5" tall

# Crochet Cat Bed

Materials:

S hook (19.00mm) – and YES.

Yarn needle

Approximately 140 yards of Loops & Threads Chunky (<6 skeins). Sample shown in "Oatmeal" (currently sold out online, but my store had plenty). Loops & Threads Chunky is a #6 super bulky yarn, HOWEVER, if you are substituting, Tecommend using a #7 Jumbo yarn.

Stitch marker or bobby pin

Gauge:

Your first 4 rounds should measure 7" across.

Abbreviations Used:

MC (magic circle) – view my tutorial here

CH (chain)

ST/STS (stitch/stitches)

SL ST (slip stitch)

SC (single crochet)

HDC (half double crochet)

Special Terminology:

3rd Loop – Some rows call for the stitches to be completed in the "3rd loop". Instead of putting your HDC in the top loops, reach your hook past the back loop where you'll find a 3rd loop on the side of the stitch. Insert your hook there to create your HDC. This forces both of the top loops to rest on the front of your project, creating a ribbing effect. In other patterns it is also referred to as a Camel Stitch or RibHDC.

Notes:

(1) This pattern is written in American Standard terms.

(2) This pattern is worked mostly in a seamless round. At Round 10, you will chain and turn, and then continue on in a seamless round in the opposite direction. This is all noted in the pattern.

(3) Starting CHs do not count as stitches.

## How To Make It Larger:

It's relatively simple, so hopefully my explanation won't sound toocomplicated. What you'll want to do is continue increasing your base until it's about 1-2 inches smaller than the size you want the bed to be. On the very last repeat of the last round you did, use SC instead of HDC for all but the last two stitches; use slip stitches for the final two stitches. (This is the equivalent of Round 9 in the pattern.) So for instance, if you did 10 increase rounds, your 10th round would be:

(2 HDC in next, 1 HDC in each of the next 8 STS) 7 times. 2 SC in next, 1 SC in each of the next 6 STS, 1 SL ST in each of the next 2 STS. (80)

Then, CH1 and turn, and do a final increase round in HDC (this is the equivalent of Round 10 in the pattern). Continue on with Round 11 and follow the pattern as written (your stitch counts will be different).

To begin:

Using S Hook, make a magic circle.

Round 1: CH1. 8 HDC in MC. (8)

Round 2: 2 HDC in each ST around. (16)

Round 3: (2 HDC in next, 1 HDC in next) around. (24)

Round 4: (2 HDC in next, 1 HDC in each of the next 2 STS) around. (32)

Round 5: (2 HDC in next, 1 HDC in each of the next 3 STS) around. (40)

Round 6: (2 HDC in next, 1 HDC in each of the next 4 STS) around. (48)

Round 7: (2 HDC in next, 1 HDC in each of the next 5 STS) around.

(56)

Round 8: (2 HDC in next, 1 HDC in each of the next 6 STS) around. (64)

Round 9: (2 HDC in next, 1 HDC in each of the next 7 STS) 7 times. 2 SC in next, 1 SC in each of the next 5 STS, 1 SL ST in each of the next 2 STS. (72)

Note: The end of round 9 should smooth down your round to blend in, instead of ending with the jagged edge that working a seamless round causes. This will enable us to chain up in the next round, turn our work, and begin working seamlessly in the other direction.

Round 10: CH1, turn your work. (2 HDC in next, 1 HDC in each of the next 8 STS) around. Do not join. (80)

Rounds 11-14: In 3rd loops, HDC in each ST around. (80)

Round 15: In 3rd loops, SC in each of the next 75 STS. SL ST in 3rd loops of each of the next 5 STS. (80)

Fasten off and weave in all ends.

# Super Big Chunky Crochet Yarn Cat Bed

Materials Used

–Super Big Chunky Yarn – Jumbo Weight 7 – That's big! (approximately 32oz for 1 bed)

–Crochet Hook – 30mm (or use your hands as a hook.

Crochet Pattern

This crochet pattern works in rounds, not rows. This means you continue to build on top of the previous row without stopping.

Make a magic ring

Round 1: sc 6 into ring, pull tail to tighten ring (6 sts)

Round 2: 2sc in each st (12 sts)

Round 3: <1sc, 2sc in next>, 5 times (18 sts)

Round 4: <1sc in next 2 sts, 2sc in next>, 6 times (24 sts)

Round 5-6: 1 sc in each st (24 sts), sl st in final st.

Tie off and weave in ends.

You're done! But….

## Crochet Cat Bed

Make a magic ring

Round 1: sc 6 into ring, pull tail to tighten ring (6 sts)

Round 2: 2sc in each st (12 sts)

Round 3: <1sc, 2sc in next> 5 times (18 sts)

Round 4: <1sc in next 2 sts, 2sc in next> 6 times (24 sts)

Round 5: <1sc in next 3 sts, 2sc in next> 6 times (30 sts)

Round 6-7: 1 sc in each st (30 sts), sl st in final st.

Tie off and weave in ends.

# Crochet Cat Bed for a Comfy Kitty Nap

Materials:

-9 skeins of Loops & Threads "Chunky" Heather Gray. (Approximately 240 yards total)

-US Q(15.75mm) hook

-Scissors

-Tapestry needle

Directions:

Abbreviations used:

HDC-Half double crochet

DC: Double Crochet

SS: Slip stitch

MC: Magic circle

Crochet Cat Bed

Note: The first chain two of every round does not count as a stitch.

1. Work 12 DC into magic circle, SS to first DC to join. (12)

2. Chain 2. DC 2 in same stitch and in each stitch around. SS to first

DC to join. (24)

3. Chain 2. 2DC in same stitch. *DC in next 2 stitches, 2DC in next stitch; repeating from* to end. SS to beginning DC to join. (32)

4. Chain 2. 2DC in same stitch. *DC in next 3 stitches, 2DC in next stitch; repeating from* to end. SS to beginning DC to join. (40)

5. Chain 2. 2DC in same stitch. *DC in next 4 stitches, 2DC in next stitch; repeating from*, to end. SS to beginning DC to join. (48)

6. Chain 2. 2DC in same stitch. *DC in next 4 stitches, 2DC in next stitch; repeating from* to end. SS to first DC to join. (56)

7. Chain 2. HDC into front loop of same stitch. HDC into front loop of each stitch around. SS to first HDC.

8. Chain 2. HDC into same stitch and each stitch around. SS to initial HDC to join. Tie off and weave in ends.

9. Repeat Row 8 till desired height.

Liner:

Repeat rows 1-5 and tie off. Place inside cat bed.

Crochet Cat Bed

If you want to make the bed larger, simply continue with sequence of stitches after row 6 (ex: row 7a would be- 2DC in one stitch, DC in next 5 Stitches), adding one more DC between every 2DC each round you increase.

# Cozy Crochet Cat Bed

Before you begin, run the wool through a lightly closed hand several times. Hold the wool in one hand and gently pull it through with the other. This will compress the fibers and help the roving to pass though the crochet loops without breaking.

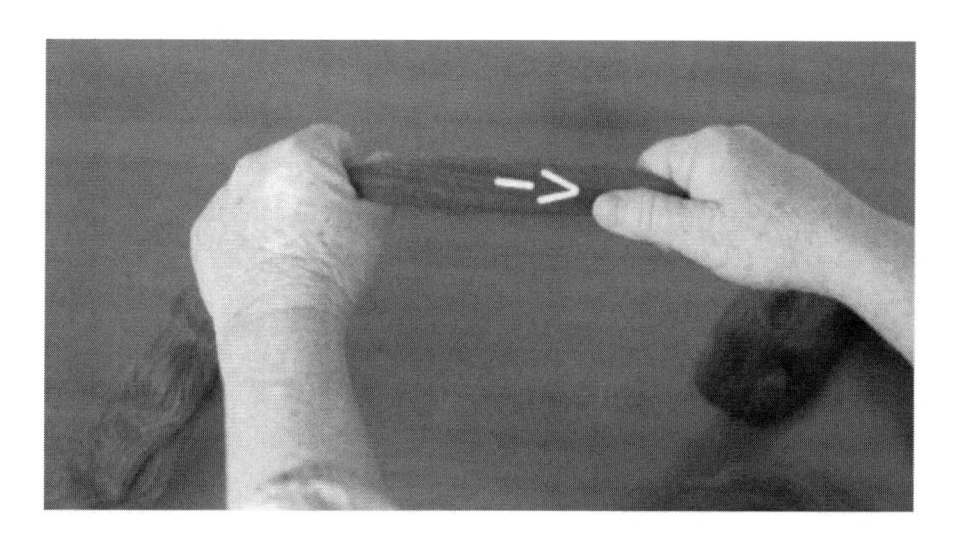

Finger crochet stitches are exactly the same as regular crochet. The only difference is that you will need to reach through the loops and grab the working yarn – in this case roving – with your middle and index fingers to pull them through.

Start by chaining 2 in the end of the roving.

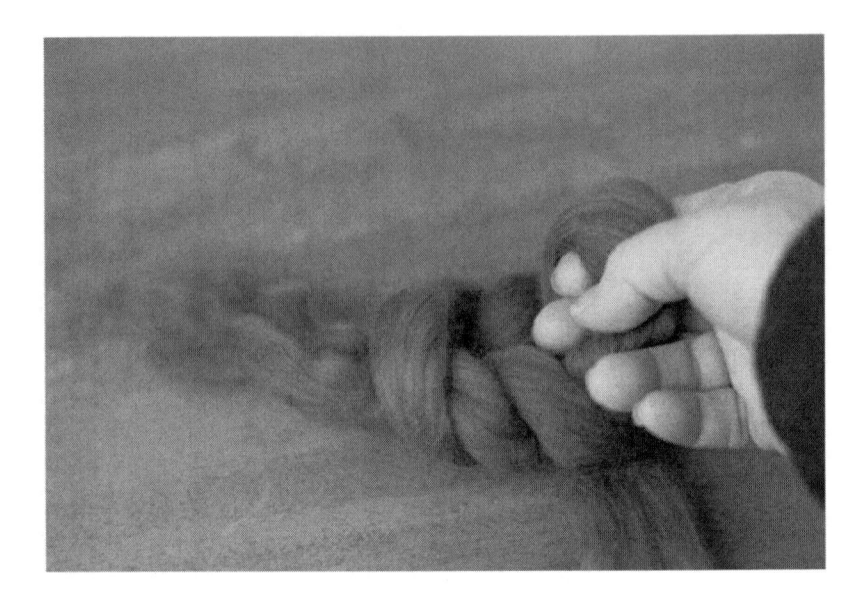

Reach through the loop created by the 2nd chain.

While keeping the loop on your finger, reach through the hole from the 1st chain.

Pull the working roving through. Keep both loops on your finger and grab the working roving.

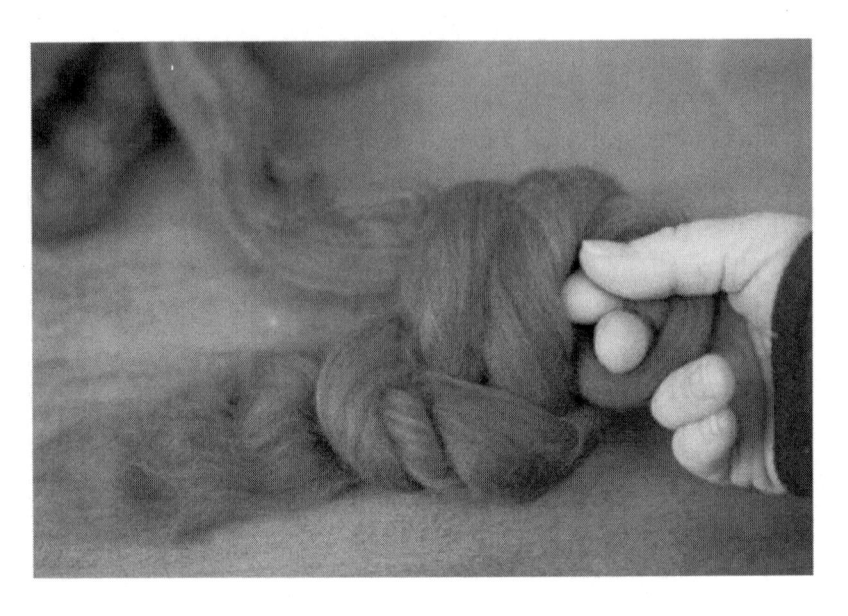

Pull it through both loops on your finger. This creates one single crochet stitch (SC). Make 5 more SC in the same hole (6 SC total).

Round 2: Using the same technique, make 2 SC in each of the SC from the 1st round, for a total of 12 SC.

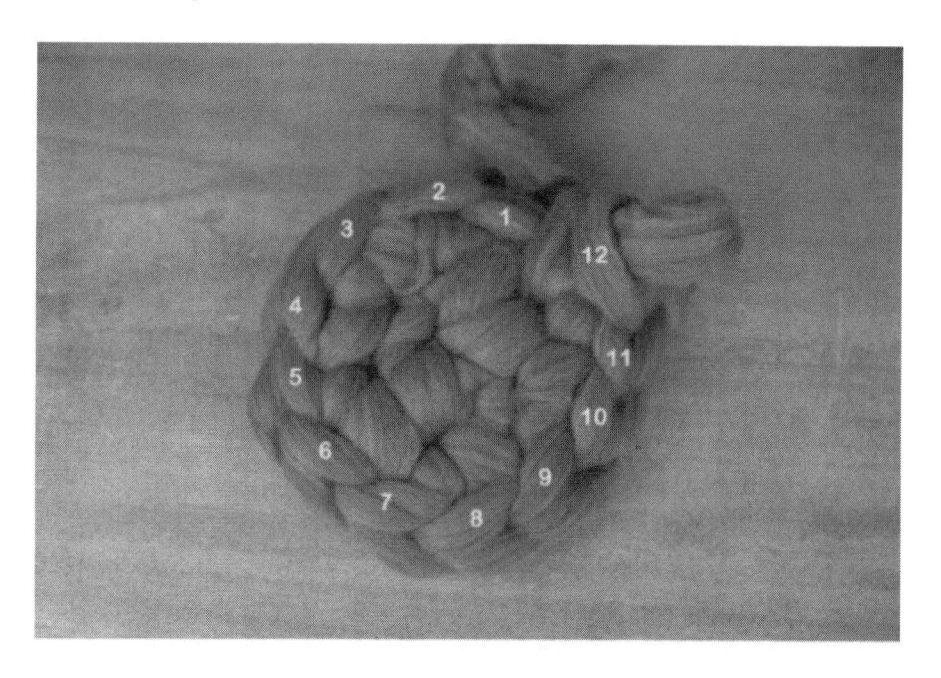

Reach through the loop to make a single chain by pulling the roving through.

# Crochet Cat Bed

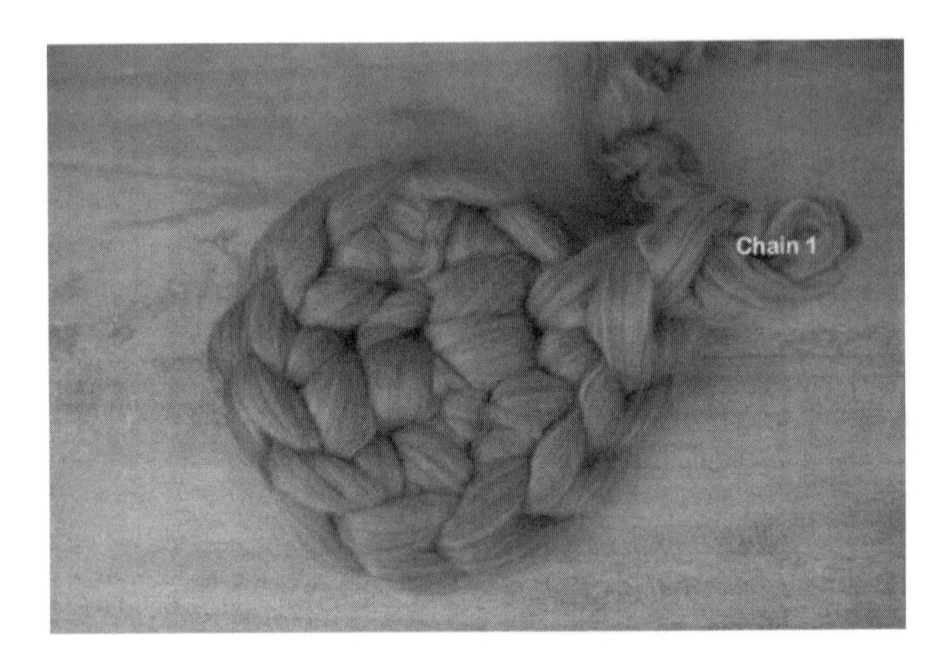

Continue to make 2 SC in each stitch as done in round 2, ending with a single chain, until your bed is the size desired.

Now it's time to build the walls. Continue around with a single crochet in each instead of the double crochets. This will cause the sides to rise forming a nice basket shape for Kitty to snuggle in.

Crochet Cat Bed

Make 3 or 4 rounds and then finish off with a slip stitch. Break the roving and gently weave the ends in, hiding them within the previous chains.

# Crochet Cat Bed

This makes a very soft and cosy bed for a cat or small dog. This project is not well suited for an overly playful pet as the roving itself is easily shredded by rambunctious claws. But if your mature cat is looking for a special place to curl up, this will certainly make him happy!

# Perfect Crocheted Cat Bed

what you'll need

600 grams of Super Bulky Yarn (approximately 950 yards).

10 mm crochet hook

Tapestry needle

pattern:

**You will hold the yarn double throughout the construction of the bed.

First we will make the bottom of the bed, then the sides and then the inside of the bed where your cat will sleep.

the bottom:

Holding yarn double, sc 6 in magic ring (6)

*inc * repeat around (12)

*sc, inc* repeat (18)

*sc 2, inc* repeat (24)

*sc 3, inc* repeat (30)

*sc 4, inc* repeat (36)

*sc 5, inc * repeat (42)

*sc 6, inc * repeat (48)

*sc 7, inc * repeat (54)

*sc 8, inc * repeat (60)

*sc 9, inc * repeat (66)

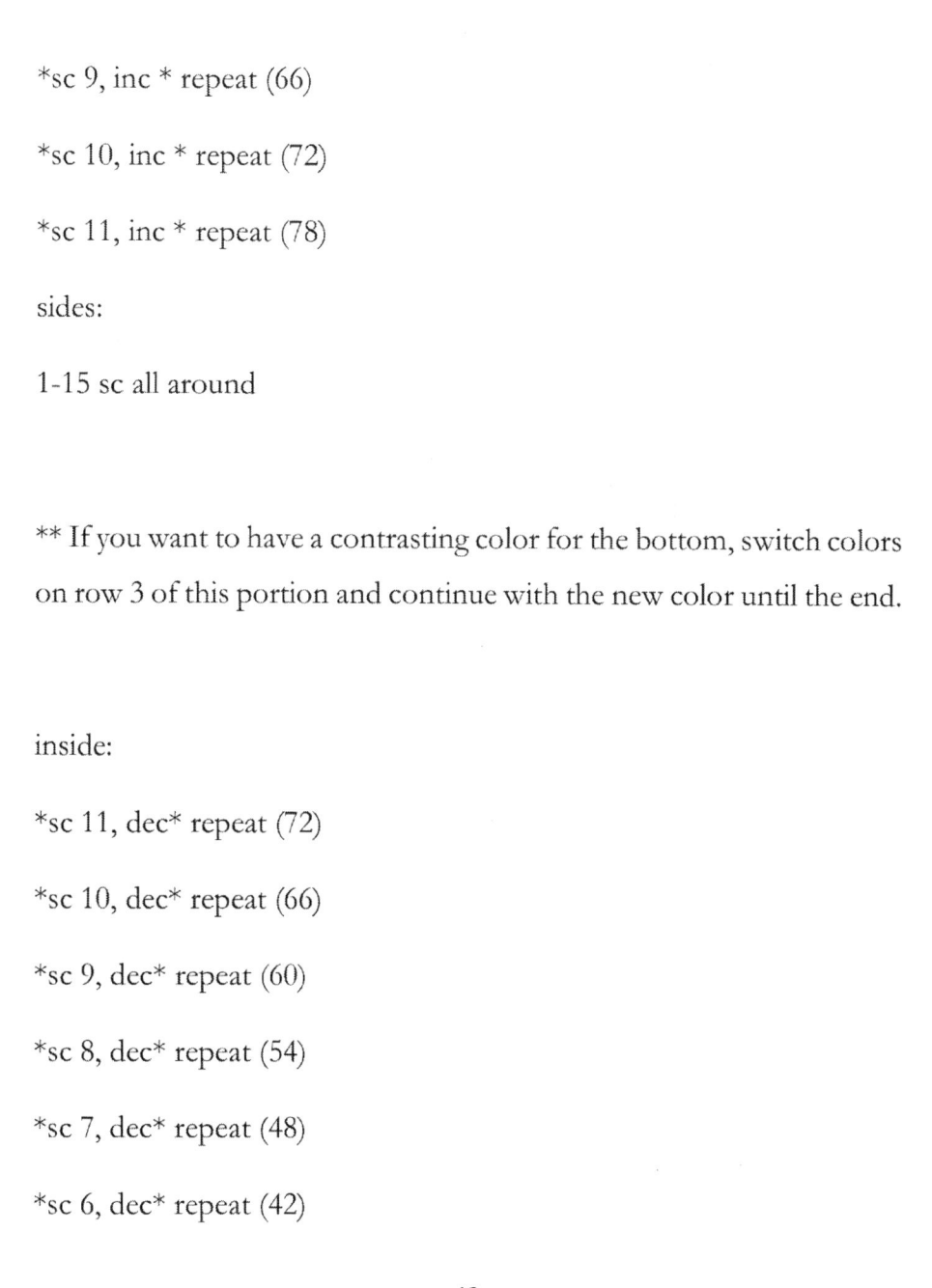

*sc 10, inc * repeat (72)

*sc 11, inc * repeat (78)

sides:

1-15 sc all around


** If you want to have a contrasting color for the bottom, switch colors on row 3 of this portion and continue with the new color until the end.


inside:

*sc 11, dec* repeat (72)

*sc 10, dec* repeat (66)

*sc 9, dec* repeat (60)

*sc 8, dec* repeat (54)

*sc 7, dec* repeat (48)

*sc 6, dec* repeat (42)

*sc 5, dec* repeat (36)

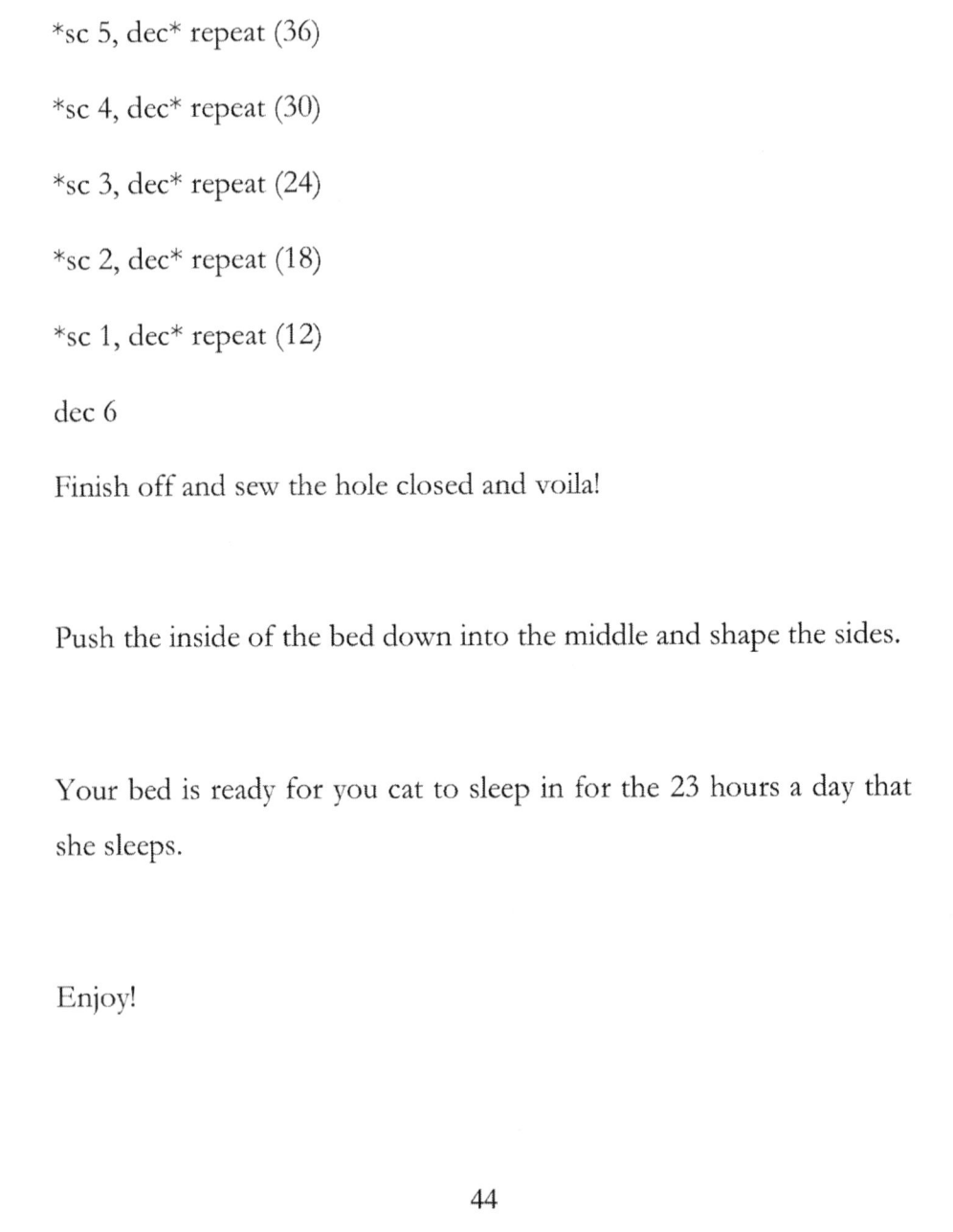

*sc 4, dec* repeat (30)

*sc 3, dec* repeat (24)

*sc 2, dec* repeat (18)

*sc 1, dec* repeat (12)

dec 6

Finish off and sew the hole closed and voila!

Push the inside of the bed down into the middle and shape the sides.

Your bed is ready for you cat to sleep in for the 23 hours a day that she sleeps.

Enjoy!

# Crochet Fluffy Dreams Pet Bed

This pet bed was made to accommodate a regular size cat but can work for kittens and small to medium dogs or other animals. It measures roughly 50 cm across including the rolled sides (red line on the photo) and 38 cm between the rolled sides (green line on the photo).

# Crochet Cat Bed

Materials:

- Size 8 mm crochet hook
- Bulky or super bulky weight yarn that yields required gauge (amounts may differ depending on the brand. For this project about 400 g of yarn was used).
- Synthetic polyester stuffing or any stuffing that can withstand washing
- Large sewing needle that can accommodate the matching yarn.

Gauge:

9 single crochet stitches - 10 cm

5 single crochet rows - 10 cm

Description:

This pet bed is worked in a circle in rows of single crochet stitches. It consists of two parts – the foundation and the side.

Foundation:

The foundation part is worked in a circle with regular increases to create a desired shape.

R0:     Crochet 6 CH ST and SL ST in the first CH ST to close the ring.

R1:     Crochet 3 CH ST and crochet the following in the ring: 1 SC, *2 CH ST, 2 SC*, repeat from * to * 5 more times, 2 CH ST, SL ST to join the first SC and close the ring. There should be 6 segments (1 segment of 3 CH ST and 1 SC and 5 segments of 2 SC stitches) separated by 2 CS stitches in this row.

R2:     Crochet 3 CH ST, 1 SC in the base of the 3 CH ST, 1 SC in the SC of the previous row, 1 SC in the 2 CH ST of the previous row, *2 CH ST, 1 SC in the 2 CH of the previous row, 2 SC in the 2 SC of the previous row, 1 SC in the 2 CH of the previous row*. Repeat from * to * 4 more times, 2 CH ST, SL ST to join the first SC and close the ring. There should be 6 segments (1 segment of 3 CH ST and 3 SC and 5 segments of 4 SC stitches) separated by 2 CH stitches.

R3-10: Continue working in a similar manner, adding 2 SC for each of the 6 segments, separated by 2 CH ST.

R11: Add 2 SC for each of the 6 segments, which will result in 22 SC in each of the 5 segments and 21 SC in the segment with 3 CH ST (3 CH ST at the beginning of the row and 131 SC). DO NOT add 2 CH ST between segments in this row. At this point the bed foundation should measure about 44 cm in diameter.

Side:

The pet bed side part is worked in a circle without increases to create a desired shape.

R12: Crochet 3 CH ST and 131 BPSC above the SC of the previous row. BPSC will mark the beginning of the side part.

R13-23: Crochet 3 CH ST and 131 SC above the SC of the previous rows. Fasten off and break yarn. Weave in the ends. Once finished crocheting, the side should be about 24 cm in height.

Crochet Cat Bed

This is how the pet bed looks in the process of being crocheted:

This is how the pet bed looks when crocheting is finalized:

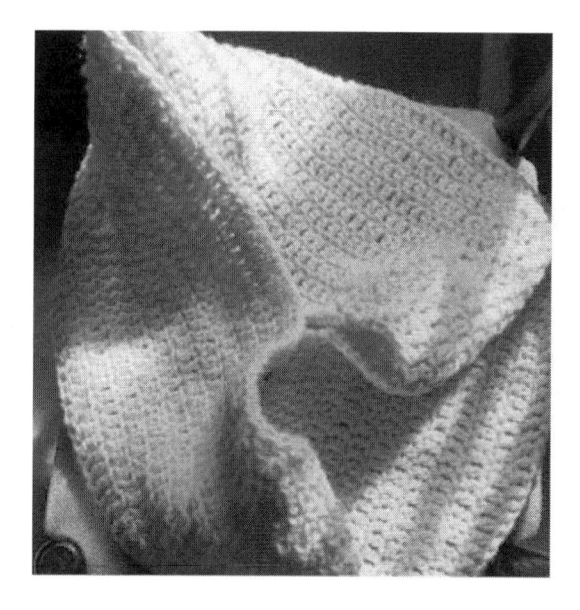

## Assembly:

Lay the pet bed on a flat surface. Thread the needle with matching yarn and start sewing the top of the side to the R11 of the foundation, so that the resulting seam is on the inside of the pet bed. As you continue sewing, start stuffing the resulting hollow tube with stuffing of your choice. Ensure the ends of the side align with stitches of R11. Continue stuffing to achieve the desired look and feel of the pet bed. Once you complete stuffing, secure the thread, cut off the end and weave in the end.

Should you stuff it before or after felting? Opinions differ. To ensure the best result, you can assemble and stuff the pet bed prior to felting, but leave a little opening in the seam between the side and the foundation if there is a significant change in the size after felting and you need to add or remove stuffing.

This is how the pet bed looks after it is stuffed, washed and dried:

Crochet Cat Bed

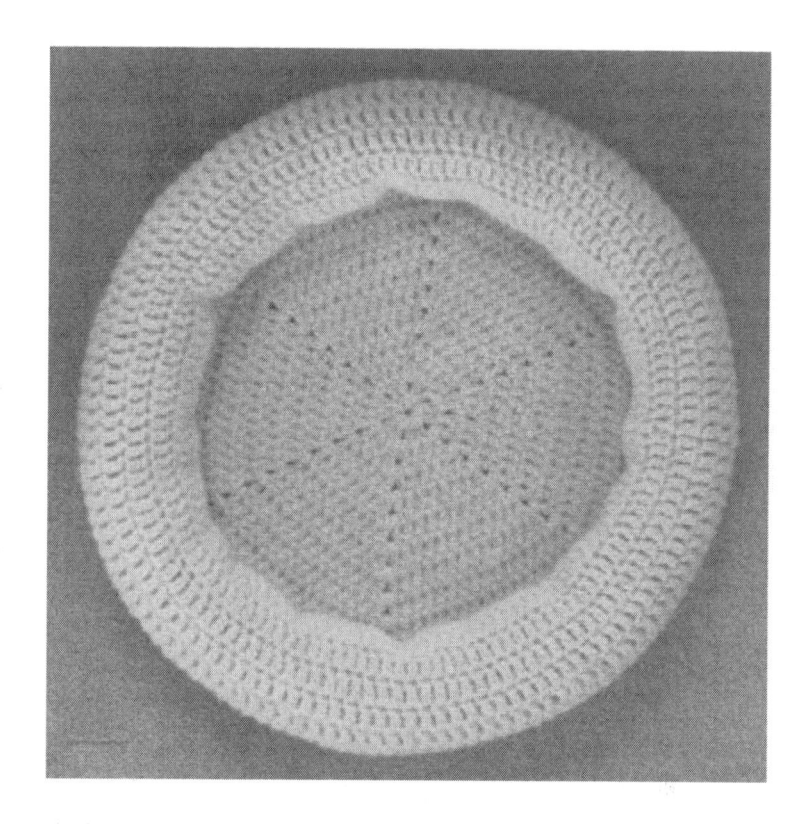

Abbreviations (US version):

BPSC   back post single crochet

CH ST  chain stitch

R      row

SC     single crochet

SL ST  slip stitch

# Crochet Cat Cave

Equipment

Crochet Hook - Size P

Materials

Chunky Caron Cakes Yarn

10" Steel Hoop

Instructions

Create a slip knot with a 3-4" tail. Bring the yarn from the center of the ball around the hoop. Create a single crochet stitch around the hoop.

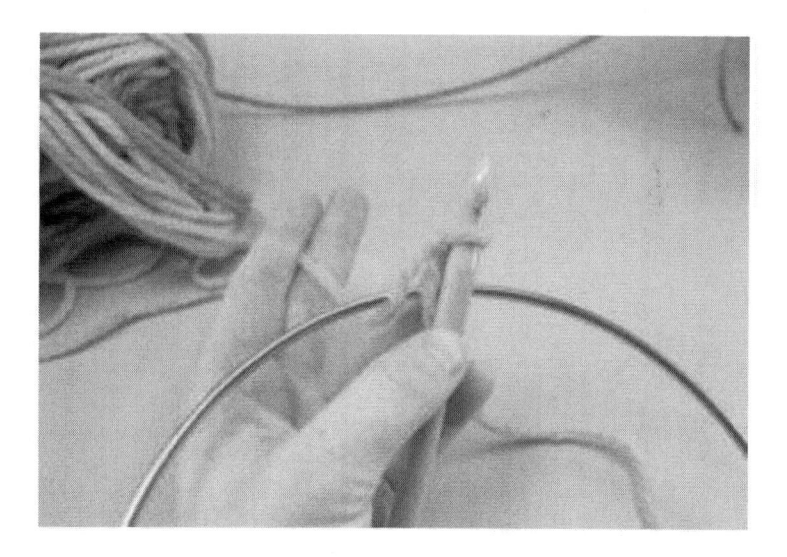

Continue making single crochet stitches around the hoop.

Crochet Cat Bed

Once you reach the first stitch you made, join the last with a slip stitch to close the round.

You don't need to join rounds, simply continue to crochet into the next stitch no matter which round it is from. Working this way will make the fabric grow in a spiral fashion that won't show any seams.

Once the crochet cat cave has enough length, finish the last round with a few slip stitches to even out the end. Tie off the yarn and weave in the end.

Printed in Great Britain
by Amazon